A Woman with a Minute...

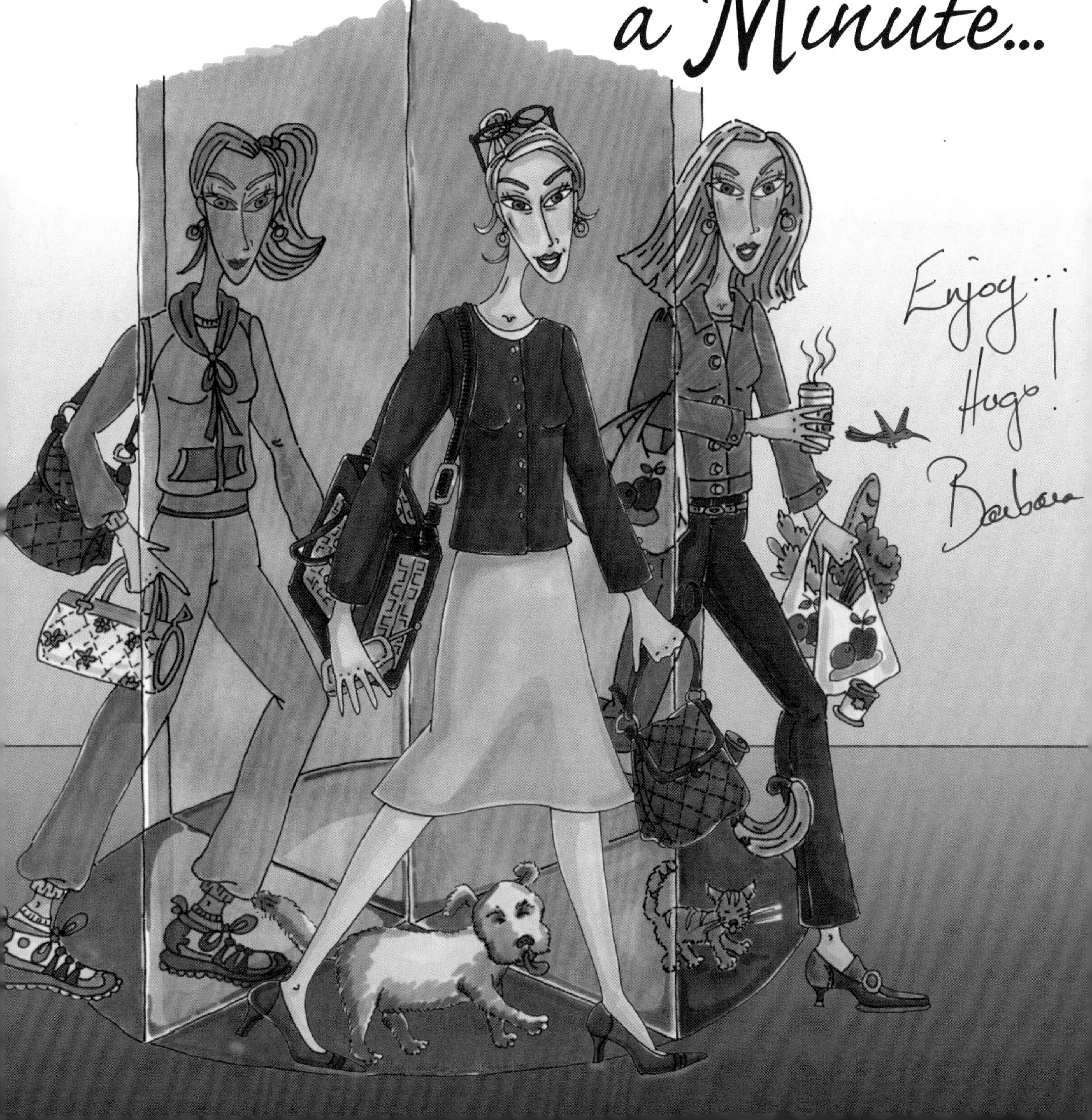

Enjoy...
Hugo!
Barbara

ISBN #978-09746722-1-2

Illustration by Anita Bartlett

Text design by Loneta Showell

Editing by Michelle Asakawa, Valari Burger and Barb Weiman

Published by IntelligentRisking™, Inc.

Printed in Canada

www.IntelligentRisking.com

A Woman with a Minute...

I would like to acknowledge and thank Nick, Joey and Connor for their unwavering love, faith and support. Thank you for believing in me and my mountain. I'm very lucky to have the three of you in my life. A special thanks to Scandi and Pounder for teaching all of us about unconditional love.

Few climbs are solo so I would also like to thank the rest of my climbing team: Anita, Barb, Brian, Cami, Dad, Debra, Diane, Doug, Grandma Miller, Laura, Leslie, Linda, Loneta, Mellie, Mom, Neal, Ruthie, Suzy, Sylvia and last but never least, Valari.

A huge thank you to Anita for taking my vision and translating it into the fun illustrations I had imagined. Thank you for being amazingly easy to work with and so accepting of my "creative" input.

For her generous support, encouragement and direction I'd like to acknowledge Margaret Maupin at the unparalleled Tattered Cover. Thank you for seeing the potential in this book.

Dedication

This book is dedicated to you, the reader,
and all of the fabulous women out there
who are working magic with every minute.

Please give yourself the credit you deserve.

Once upon a time I wondered why I was the only one who always seemed so far behind in everything. I'd ask myself over and over again, "How does everyone else do it all?" I wondered what was wrong with me because no matter how fast I went or how hard I worked I could never seem to get caught up. I was operating under the very mistaken assumption that everyone else except me was just about perfect. I started to believe that I was the only woman out there living a fragmented life - misplacing, losing and forgetting things at an astonishing rate. Yet, on the rare occasion when I would actually stop and think about it, I would realize that despite all my mistakes, I was actually getting an amazing number of things done.

At this point I started asking other women about their days. I found that once we got past the superficial, "I'm fine, my job is wonderful and my children are perfect.", almost everyone's life was similar to mine. No matter the women's nationality, whether or not they had children, whether or not they worked outside of the home, whether or not they were married; all of us had way too much to do, not enough time to do it and no matter how much we got done, we all felt as if we were getting farther and farther behind.

Women may go about their day in a somewhat random and distracted way. At times we may go about things in a somewhat unorganized, unconventional and unorthodox way, yet somehow we seem to get an absolutely amazing amount accomplished. We are proof that the Chaos Theory works.

The moral of this story is that no one is perfect. In fact, perfection is positively boring and leaves no room for excitement and spontaneity. Today's woman lives a demanding life and each of us needs to realize we are doing an exceptional job. We are sharp, smart and sophisticated women who are making it happen. So, let's give ourselves credit and start living happily (not perfectly) ever after!

A Woman with a Minute...

will want to sit down
in her favorite chair.

However, first she may want to...

...get a cup of coffee. If there isn't any coffee ready she'll start to make some. That's when she'll see the notes.

They will remind her to deliver the soup to her sick friend and that she still needs to make something for the bake sale today. She'll secretly wish that she would have simply ordered something from the bakery.

As the coffee brews, she'll look for a gourmet cookie recipe. Settling for the recipe on the back of the chocolate chip bag she'll realize that she needs her glasses to read it. She'll start searching for them. As she sees her reflection in the microwave she'll realize that they were on top of her head the whole time.

As she reads the recipe she'll decide to start getting out the ingredients.

If she can't find all the ingredients, that will remind her that there are still some groceries in the car.

On her way to the garage
she'll walk past the
laundry room and decide
to throw some clothes
into the washer.

When the light in the garage goes out,
she'll change the bulb, which is
when she may see the drill.

The drill will remind her that the latch on the back door is loose.

As she's tightening the latch the phone will probably ring. If it does, she'll run into the house to answer it.

If the phone is missing she'll
    follow the ringing sound to find it.

As she searches for the phone she'll think
about how she should call her mom. When
she finds the phone, the call will be a reminder for the
fundraising dinner she's to attend that evening.

She may also find the TV remote and her missing charm bracelet, the one she got on her birthday. That will remind her of her friend's upcoming birthday and that she needs to get her present into the mail today. She'll go look for the gift she purchased weeks ago.

Once she finds the present
she'll head to the
basement to wrap it.

As she starts wrapping the present she'll need scissors. If she can't find them, she'll go back upstairs to look for them.

Once she gets to the kitchen she may wonder, "Why did I come up here?" That's when she'll see the coffee pot, which will remind her that she wanted a cup of coffee. Since it's cold she'll put a cup in the microwave.

While she's in the kitchen she'll start making the cookies. After she's put them into the oven to bake she'll be tempted to lick the spoon. She'll probably be reminded of her diet and lick it anyway, promising herself she'll workout later.

With the cookies in the oven she'll head
back to her chair with a hot cup of coffee.
She'll kick off her shoes, as
cute as they are, they
have never been very
comfortable.

As she sets the coffee cup down
on the table she may hear,
"You've got mail." That
will remind her that
she hasn't checked any
of her e-mails, so
she'll go to her desk.

As she's reading her e-mails, she'll hear a beep coming from her cell phone, letting her know that the battery is low, so she'll put it into the charger. As she does, she may notice the stack of mail which will remind her that she needs to pay bills.

To make sure she avoids any late charges, she'll probably start writing checks. Once she's done she'll look for stamps. This is when she'll find the scissors. They will remind her of the present she needs to finish wrapping, so she'll head back down to the basement.

After she's finished wrapping the present she'll put on a mailing label, which will remind her she needs postage, so...

she'll go all the way back upstairs to look for stamps.

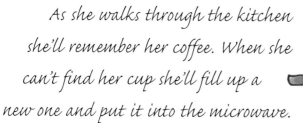

As she walks through the kitchen she'll remember her coffee. When she can't find her cup she'll fill up a new one and put it into the microwave.

That's when the timer will go off for the cookies. She'll check them and decide they need a few more minutes.

With the cookies back in the oven she'll head to her chair with a new cup of coffee. That's when she'll pick up the report, which will remind her that she wanted to print out an extra copy. So, she'll go back to her desk.

As she starts to print out the extra copy of the report she'll see the bills, and start looking for the stamps again.

That's when she may smell
something which will
remind her that she forgot
all about the cookies,
so she'll run
into the kitchen.

The burnt cookies will make her want to kick herself for
not ordering from the bakery. She begins to wonder
if anyone will notice if she doesn't bring
anything. Then her conscience will
take over and she'll make a note to
call the bakery. She may feel a little
guilty about not making something
herself so she'll plan
to take a tray for the cookies
in hopes that they'll look more
like homemade.

She'll turn on the water in the sink and put the cookie sheet in to soak so that it'll be
easier to wash later. That's when the doorbell will ring and she'll run to answer it.

If it's a neighbor circulating a petition they'll discuss the need for everyone to take action. Feeling like she should get more involved she'll agree to help by getting more signatures. Then she'll go back to the kitchen.

She knew she should have ordered from the bakery!!!

Just as she finishes mopping the floor she'll hear the alarm on her computer reminding her that it's time to get ready for her board meeting.

So, she'll run upstairs to change.

That's when she'll remember that she had dropped off her favorite suit at the cleaners

requesting overnight service and forgot to pick it up. She'll look for something else to wear.

Once she's ready to go,
she'll look for her car keys.

If they aren't in her bag, she'll look through the pockets of her coats in the hall closet.

As she's looking she may come across a stack of books that she has never finished reading. If she does she'll push them a little farther back into the closet.

Once she finds her keys she'll grab the soup, the tray, the package, the bills, her workout bag, her laptop and the reports.

Then she'll head out to the car. When she walks past the laundry room, she'll think about the clothes in the washer.

She'll probably run back into the house to put the clothes into the dryer.

Before she backs out of the driveway, she'll remember that she needs to order cookies from the bakery. So, she'll look for her cell phone and remember that she left it in the charger. She'll run back into the house again.

As she walks in she'll notice the flowers in the vase need water, so she'll take them into the kitchen with her.

Once she's in the kitchen she'll remember that she never got that cup of coffee. She'll put a to-go cup into the microwave.

So that she doesn't waste sixty seconds she'll go to get her cell phone out of the charger. When she picks it up she'll notice the time, which will remind her she'd better leave for her meeting.

As she goes out the front door she may walk past her favorite chair and smile wistfully.

Since she doesn't have time to run her errands she'll head straight to her meeting. Once the update begins she'll blind everyone with her brilliant, succinct analysis of the current situation as she covers every possible contingency, financial scenario and anticipated reaction.

She'll leave the meeting focused on her success until she reaches her car. That's when she'll notice her workout bag, which will remind her that she hasn't exercised all week.

Feeling guilty, she'll drive straight to the gym. As soon as she changes into her sweats a friend may ask her how the bake sale went. That will remind her that she hasn't picked up the cookies from the bakery and it closes in ten minutes. With no time left to workout, she'll run to the bakery.

When she walks into the bakery the smell of baking bread will remind her of home and that she needs to call her mom.

She'll call her mom from the car. If she gets so involved in the conversation that she drives right past the bake sale, she'll turn around and go back.

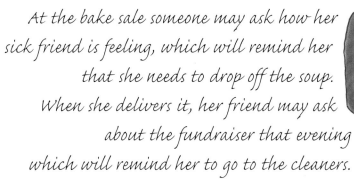

Since she didn't have time for lunch she'll be starving and tempted to eat all the cookies. However, remembering her diet she'll keep only a few for herself. The rest she'll take out of the bakery box and put on the tray.

At the bake sale someone may ask how her sick friend is feeling, which will remind her that she needs to drop off the soup. When she delivers it, her friend may ask about the fundraiser that evening which will remind her to go to the cleaners.

As she's picking up her cleaning, the owner may mention that her suit has been ready for several days, suggesting that she only request "rush service" if she needs it. Since they are always so accommodating, she'll feel badly and give them all the cookies she had kept for herself.

As she pays for her dry cleaning she'll be reminded to mail the bills and the birthday present.

Since the mail box is right next to a coffee shop she'll decide to run in and treat herself to a tall, non-fat, sugar-free vanilla latte with an extra shot of espresso.

Seeing the line, she may decide not to go in. That's when she'll notice the new little boutique next door. That will remind her of the fundraiser and that she really doesn't have anything quite right to wear.

So, she may. . .

...go shopping

When the shop starts
closing she'll
realize it's
time to head
straight home.

When she finally gets home she'll immediately
start getting ready for the fundraiser.

Once she's dressed
all she'll want to do is sit down in her favorite chair.

However, first she may want to...

...get a glass of wine.

That's when the phone will probably ring...

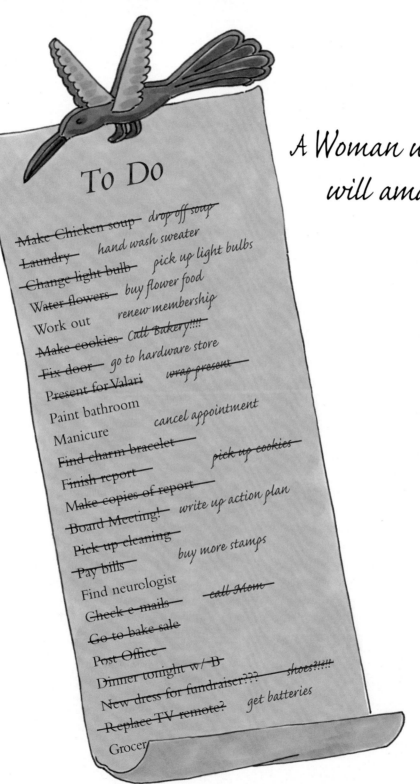

A Woman with a Minute...
will amaze you.

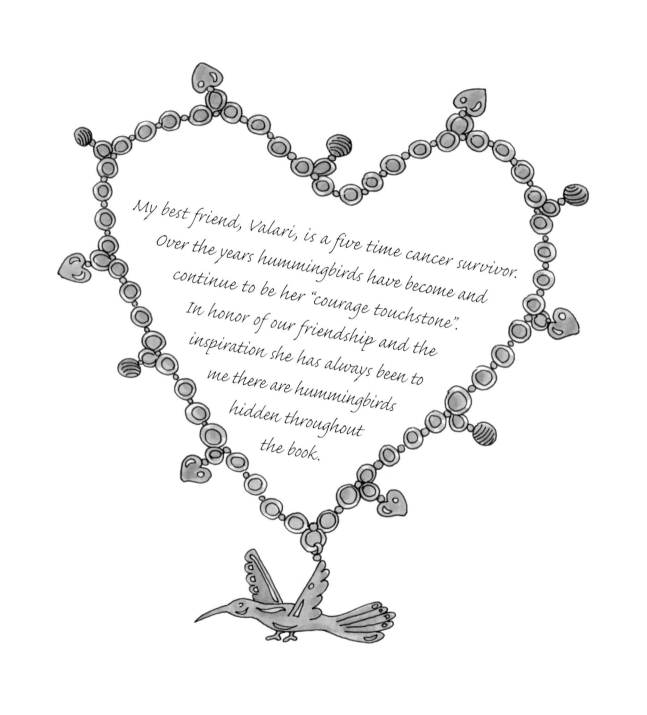

My best friend, Valari, is a five time cancer survivor. Over the years hummingbirds have become and continue to be her "courage touchstone". In honor of our friendship and the inspiration she has always been to me there are hummingbirds hidden throughout the book.

My Story

Why did I write this book? I wanted to help women, everywhere; (including myself) put their lives in perspective. I wanted women to understand and value all that they do in a day. I believe that it's important that we stop holding ourselves up to an unrealistic and ridiculous standard of perfection. It's time to let go of the craziness we allow ourselves to get caught up in and lighten up, a lesson I learned in an interesting way.

About a year ago, I had a week that really scared me. At the end of seven days I had lost a 2-carat diamond ring, a credit card, my driver's license and my cell phone twice. I had been worried about my forgetfulness for some time, but now it was time to get serious, so I decided to see a neurologist. I had to face up to whatever terrible disease was stealing my mind.

I, of course, researched and found one of the best neurologists in the Denver area. She asked me to take a number of sophisticated tests, which all came back normal. That's when she asked me to describe my life. I told her I was a single mom with three sons. We had a kitten and a dog named Pounder who had just undergone extensive reconstructive surgery on his leg.

She asked about my work. I told her that I worked full time from home, that I traveled a fair bit and that I was doing research and writing a book on women and intelligent risk taking. Then she asked what I did in my spare time. I asked her to define "spare time." She described it as any time left over when I wasn't sleeping. I told her I was involved in the boy's school, their activities and their sports. She asked about my passions. I shared that I was a Wish Grantor for the Make-A-Wish Foundation and that I loved to climb plus I had just become a paragliding pilot.

When she inquired about how old my sons were I simply opened the door for her to see for herself. Since I hadn't found anyone brave enough to watch them that day, I had been forced to bring them with me.

Joey (10) had climbed up on the windowsill and was looking upside-down into the aquarium making bizarre faces and noises at the fish. Nick (12) was launching a full-scale military assault with at least 100 G.I.Joe's that he had set up on the chairs, tables and floor. Connor (13) had draped himself across the couch in torn-up black clothes, reading a skater magazine and listening to Heavy Metal music through his headphones. His music was so loud that we could hear it all the way back in the examination room.

Fortunately for me the neurologist had a sense of humor. She looked at me and told me I had two options; lose the kids or simplify my life. I have tried both with mediocre success.

To this day my ring is still missing. I found my credit card at Krispy Kreme Doughnuts when I had driven through for a quick doughnut on my way to a work-out. My driver's license turned up at the gym (I had to use it to get in since I couldn't find my membership card). I called my own cell phone just to see if anyone would answer it. Mark, from the express lane at the grocery store, said "Hello". He remembered me clearly; I was the lady with 16 items in the line for 10 items or fewer. He said he also had found my membership card to the gym.

Two days after I had recovered my cell phone, I got a call in my office. The caller ID said the number was the same as my cell phone. Wondering why my caller ID wasn't working I picked up the call. It turned out that some honest soul was calling me from my own cell phone. It turned out that she'd found it in the parking lot of my son's school. This was quite a surprise since I had not yet realized that I had lost it.

I have truly tried my neurologist's options. I've tried losing the boys several times, but they keep finding their way back home. And, I've tried to simplify my life. That hasn't gone very well either, as every day things seem to get more complicated with more demands.

I travel all over the world lecturing and consulting on IntelligentRisking. For the past ten years I have focused on women and risk. I set out to discover why intelligent, capable women are so often reluctant to take the risks required for success. Although I arrived at no simple answers, I have uncovered that a unique phenomenon takes place with women. We know intellectually that we are talented and that we want our talents, strengths and success to be valued by others. Yet, too often, we are the ones who ignore our strengths, play down our successes, focus on our mistakes, devalue our own accomplishments, and refuse to give ourselves the credit we've earned which in turn undermines our self-confidence. We constantly hold ourselves up to an unrealistic standard of perfection and find ourselves lacking. If we have 100 things on our 'To Do List' and get 95 done, most of us will still go to bed frustrated by what we didn't get done.

I see this phenomenon in myself and in other women so I decided to write two books to help women make a shift; this book which takes a fun light-hearted approach and a second book, IntelligentRisking and Women, which takes a more serious look at how to take intelligent risks.

My challenge (to all of us) is that we start giving ourselves credit, acknowledge how very talented we are and then go take those risks that will make a difference in our lives and in the lives of others.

IntelligentRisking for Women   Excerpt

The Crux Move

My fingers are jammed into a tiny crack as I press the edge of my climbing shoe against a sliver of rock. This route is at the upper end of my skill range; a successful climb here will take me to the next level in my ability. I have been climbing strong today, but now I'm approaching the most important and difficult part of the climb. Navigate this overhang and I will make it to the top. Misjudge it and the best I can hope for is to escape unscathed and call it a day. I'm at the pivotal point of any climb…known as the crux move.

I feel my right foot slipping. I shift my weight to rebalance. What was I thinking picking a route this difficult? It's pointless to ask the mountain to be easier; I must become a better climber. Still, this space between comfort and challenge is hard.

I stop, take some deep breaths, and assess my situation. I'm two hundred feet above the ground with the full weight of my body supported by a quarter inch of granite. The muscles in my calf are starting to quiver. Elvis is alive and his moves are in my leg. I'm under an overhang that juts out into eternity. My heart races when I realize the tremendous amount of faith I've placed in my own abilities.

Time stands still as I try to cut a deal with this rock. Adrenaline races through my body; my lips and mouth are dry. Strategy is as critical as execution. Quickly I determine the next few moves that will get me through the crux. This is a chess game played on a granite board with a stopwatch ticking. I move into position under the roof.

I waver for an instant, and for the first time wonder if I'm in over my head. In that moment of self-doubt, I hear a haunting whisper from the monster that hides in the recesses of my mind: "This is beyond you. You're not good enough—if you move you'll fall." Now that I've allowed myself to hear the monster within taunting me, I can't stop listening. The voice grows louder. "You don't have what it takes. You'd better quit." I tell myself that this voice of the monster within is only my own self-induced sabotage.

I know from past experience that even though these next few moves are risky, taking the time to indulge my doubts poses an even greater risk, an Invisible Risk. I need all the energy I have and the clock is running. Every second I waste listening to that voice, I burn up precious strength. Hesitating and 'holding on' virtually sentences me to a fall. My arms are screaming. I am balanced on a pencil-width of rock. Now I realize I can't see above the rock to find a handhold. How much more difficult can this get? I must make a "blind move" or the climb ends here. Somehow, I've got to find the guts to leave this very slim margin of safety.

If I move, I may fall, but if I don't move, I will certainly fall. The choice is mine alone. If I wait too long, my lack of strength will make the choice for me. It's true; weakness makes a coward of us all. I choose to climb. Cautiously, I remove my left hand from the crack to put some chalk on it so I can get a better grip when I make my attempt. I get that hold back and chalk up my right. Then I swing that arm as far as I can over the ledge searching for a crack, a minor indentation, a bump. Nothing. Nowhere.

I will myself to stretch farther, to become longer. Finding another centimeter I search the rock again. There it is! I've got a hold! I move my legs as far up under the overhang as they can go. I release my left hand and arch it blindly over the rock to find another hold. My feet swing out. I squeeze and pull with all my strength. An abyss of nothingness lies below. There is nothing but air under me now.

Even though I've made that move, I'm still not safe. I make a transition in my moves from sheer strength to delicate placement. I slow my breathing to a more controlled level. To keep the monster within at bay, I maintain a calm mind and stay focused. From my tenuous position, I balance and move my left leg up and over the edge, and then I place my toe into a splinter of rock. It's not much, but it's just enough to pull myself from gravity's clutches. I reach safety pausing for a moment to savor the victory. For this day I have overcome the monster and made the crux move!

Crux Moves in Life

On every climb there is a crux move, the single most difficult move on the climb. It's the point of no return. You either make the move or not; very much like the risks you have to take in life to reach your goals. The premise and the irony are the same, you have to let go of where you are to make your move. You must take risks to be safe.

Embrace your Adventure

There's no point in climbing anything if you aren't having fun. Since life doesn't seem to go out of its way to make anything easy for us, it's up to us to seize the day. As a wish grantor for the Make-A-Wish Foundation, I consider all my wish children to be special; however, as we talk about embracing your adventure I'm reminded of Katherine.

I love to make things special for the kids. Since Katherine's wish was to go to Disney World I had picked up a tiara and a magic wand for her. On her wish the Make-A-Wish office also sent along some small gifts. When she opened them we were all a little surprised that she had gotten a complete set of little girls' makeup. We were more surprised when we realized it was all "bright blue". Well we all know that girls, no matter their age, like to try on new makeup immediately and Katherine was no different.

Katherine already had on her tiara and was holding her wand, so she looked like quite a princess. Since she was suffering from a disease that was deteriorating her spine along with additional complications, she had limited dexterity with her hands and was forced to use a customized wheel chair. She asked me to help out with her "makeover."

I'm certainly not an experienced cosmetologist so we quickly had blue sparkle powder and eye shadow all over both of us. Then she asked me to do her nails with the iridescent blue nail polish. Once I finished she looked down at the manicure I had given her and frowned. Not being able to remember my name she said, "Princess Servant, you missed a spot." I fixed it, and she wheeled herself up to the full-length mirror in the hallway to survey the results of her makeover. She looked in the mirror and said, "Look out Cinderella, there's a new princess coming to town!" It was a magical moment.

A special acknowledgement
to all the exceptional children I have
had the honor and privilege of getting
to know through the Make-A-Wish Foundation.

Thank you for teaching me to
measure life in memories.

Barbara, Your Princess Servant

Contact and ordering information:
www.IntelligentRisking.com
303-779-1999